T0196445

ASSOCIATION DWELLING

ASSOCIATION DWELLING

a forensic look

BESS CALDWELL

ASSOCIATION DWELLING
A FORENSIC LOOK

iUniverse books may be ordered through booksellers or by contacting:

iUniverse
1663 Liberty Drive
Bloomington, IN 47403
www.iuniverse.com
1-800-Authors (1-800-288-4677)

ISBN: 978-1-4917-9597-2 (sc)
ISBN: 978-1-4917-9598-9 (e)

Library of Congress Control Number: 2016906887

Print information available on the last page.

iUniverse rev. date: 04/27/2017

Association Dwelling

All I want to do is paint my house and move in...

332

By Bess Caldwell

Contents

Foreword

Congratulations! As a first time homeowner, you have reached the decision to invest in a nonprofit Association lifestyle. You chose a two bedroom, two- bath unit. Other amenities consist of two parking spaces, heated pool, sauna area, gym, barbecue area, and in-house maintenance. You are completely sold! However, have you not yet glanced at any of the legal entities associated with a nonprofit investment lifestyle? You know, the Association Bylaws, CC&R'S and Davis-Stirling Act, city Ordinances, Office of the Secretary of State, Department of Consumer Affairs, Internal Revenue Services, as well as the non-profit status? Was that a yes or a no reply? Fantastic! Let's take a closer look!

"a look under the hood"

The Common Interest Development

A look under the hood

"Location is good" the asking price is within budget and the amenities incredible! But, why does the agent continually reference the Davis-Stirling Enactment? It would appear it is as important as the "property deed". Perhaps, this is no "ordinary" real estate purchase. Let's give this "Enactment" a more detailed look".

As an investor, are you capable of determining whether or not the non-profit Association operational decisions are in sink with California State standards, or are unregulated governance and maintenance practices the reality? There is a defined legislative process that is inseparable from a nonprofit Association investment, and Davis-Stirlings is that legislative "corner stone", the engine driving this regulatory process. This enactment represents the overarching legislative strategy for assessing and maintaining non-profit Association valuation. The narrative examines the legislative "nuts and bolts" of Davis-Stirling, and their consequential impact upon Association valuation from eight perspectives. It is the steadfast compliance of these state mandates that promote overall investment valuation. No other competing infrastructure or imposed practices can legally redefine this state authority. Again, it is the integrity of Davis-Stirling legislation that standardizes the governing, and operating practices of the non-profit Association industry. The elected Board, professional vendor, as well as the investor/Member, are all answerable to the same legislative authority. Davis-Stirling empowers the investor/Member with oversight authority pertaining to all non-profit decisions.

Only the lack of investor/Member oversight and lack of self-education of this legislation will ultimately impact outcome, and standardization of governing within this non-profit environment. For example, as an investor/Member, have you yet read the fiscal contract agreement between the Association and Managing agent as well as the required Managing agent disclosure information?

Many woes for the non-profit Association begin with the lack of such diligent oversight, allowing for self-serving goals to run counter to Davis-Stirling mandates. Such unauthorized practices can wrongfully transfer fiscal planning and decision- making authority into the hand of outside interests. Only by active engagement and literacy of state legislation can the investor/Member effectively guard against de facto, unregulated governance and management practices. Investment valuation is only maintained by steadfast compliance of Davis-Stirling. No competing contractual model within the Association can be legally substituted, nor is neutrality on the part of the investor/Member ever an option. The investor/Member must remain alert to such destabilizing practices. Therefore, it is the duty of each investor/Member to become self-educated, remain alert and engaged.

Any such unregulated and institutionalized practices must be identified and called out for what they are, unregulated de facto controls. A member who is denied access to non-profit Association records is an example of de facto control. Davis-Stirling provides the investor/Member access to such records. Another example of de facto control would consist of a Board unilaterally electing to substitute a non-profit Association pre-approved auditing process for a lesser, unapproved review process. A final example of de facto governing would consist of a Member being denied rightful access, or usage to any common area unless additional restrictions are first imposed. Keep in mind that membership to the non-profit Association is automatic and an inherent right of the investor/Member upon finalization of a sales purchase contract. From this legislative perspective of Davis-Stirling, we come to understand the difference between the unaltered inherent rights of the investor/Member, and unauthorized de-facto governing and management practices within the non-profit Association environment. Though the Association is required to elect a new Board each fiscal year, each new Board is answerable to the same legislative infrastructure of Davis-Stirling from one fiscal year to the next.

The Directors of the Board are representatives elected from among the membership to officially govern, and direct the Association fiscal affairs using only mandated methods. By contrast, the professional vendor under contractual agreement with the Association is responsible for performing duties not associated with governing, or the decision- making process. Whenever governing, and management processes are decoupled from mandated goals, methods, and timelines, fiscal problems arise, possibly impacting the Association non-profit status. Therefore, all governing and managing processes should be steadfastly anchored in the regulatory structure of Davis-Stirling, free of self-serving influences and changes.

Official filings information of the Association non-profit status and its Articles of Incorporation are registered with the Office of Secretary of State. Together, they clearly define the non- profit character and objectives. Davis-Stirling and the Association Bylaws legally define the following: Association governance duties, methods, internal mediation process, and timelines related to the budget, preparation and distribution of financial reports, auditing process, and non-profit statuses. Also defined are disclosure rights and procedures related to the election process, record keeping, foreclosure, and injunctive relief issues. It is this extraordinary body of laws that provide leverage against institutionalized practices, and promotion of investment valuation. Active involvement of the investor/Member is necessary to protect mandates and practices set forth by Davis-Stirling. Within this non-profit, regulatory structure, no entity can govern or act independently. Davis-Stirling, together with Association Bylaws, represents the only *under the hood* authority defining the Common Interest Development.

Scenarios interspersed throughout this book illustrate how a decoupling of the governing, and managing processes from the Davis-Stirling Act result in unofficial deregulations, and unauthorized de facto practices.

Scenario

Soon after Accurate Association hired Mindful Management, the Board decided to charge members a monthly usage fee of $30 for storage space located in common areas. The Board assured Members that the additional funds would be used to offset Accurate Association monthly operating expenses. Mindful Management however, advised against the Association's decision stating that while overall member dues could be increased, based on the fiscal budget, any additional usage fee aside from the budget was not permitted.

Implications: Based on the definition of "common area" of the Association, the right for potential storage space usage is already factored into ownership usage rights upon purchase. By attempting to impose an additional usage fee aside from member monthly dues, would Board's actions redefine the definition of "common area" usage as an inherent right of members? Under Davis-Stirling statutes, regular monthly assessment fees already include the right to use the common storage area without imposing any extra usage fee.

Davis-Stirling Act

Civil Code 1350 Title

This title shall be known and may be cited as the Davis-Stirling Common Interest Development Act.

Civil Code 1351 Defined Terms

As used in this title, the following terms have the following meaning:

(a) "Association" means a non-profit corporation created for the purpose of managing a common interest development.

(b) "Common area" means the entire common interest development except the separate interests therein. The estate in the common area may be a fee, a life estate, an estate for years, or any combination of the foregoing. However, the common area for a planned development may consist of mutual or reciprocal easement rights pursuant to the separate interests.

Scenario

Recreational options such as the swimming pool, hot tub, in door gym, steam room, and general indoor recreational area are among the available choices available to its members without an additional required fee. It was suggested however, by a Board Member that by monetizing these amenities would further capitalized the Association budgeted amount. After careful consideration by the Board, however, it was unanimously agreed to that an extra usage fee, in addition to the required member fee, could not be separated out and doubled charged.

Implication: It was made clear to this Board/Member however, that all amenities were accessible to the Members was an inherent right and that they were not to be separated out and charged a usage fee. Also, based on the state enactment of Davis-Sterling, the grounds and outer perimeters of the Association are characterized as "common area" environs. Therefore, it is the elected Board's responsibility to consider these regulations in their overall decision-making process.

Home Owner's Association Dwelling

"the manual"

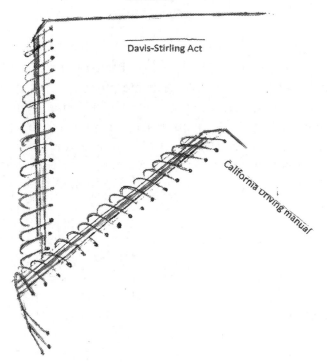

Davis-Stirling Act

California Driving manual

Homeowner's Association Dwelling

Regulatory filings

"It appears I am close to becoming a first time home owner. But wait! I must have been distracted by the hot tub and other poolside amenities when the regulatory "filings thing" was edged into the conversation. It would appear it too, is very much a part of my "care free", envisioned lifestyle. Yes, the "regulatory filings", in the form of Association Bylaws, impact the non-profit Association investment valuation ".

As an investor/owner in the Common Interest Development, can you determine whether or not Association operational practices are compatible with its 'legal filings' character? Do you understand how such a regulatory filings structure impacts investment valuation? Let's examine the non-profit concept from a "regulatory filing" perspective. Marketing tactics emphasizing onsite amenities such as the bubbling hot tub, swimming pool, barbecue facilities, and gym are powerful and persuasive visuals incentivizing the purchase decision of an investor. However, such marketing strategies only highlight physical amenities and not the unseen reality that the investor/ Member may or may not have authority pertaining to non-profit fiscal operational decisions, with or without professional guidance.

This authoritative document is pre-structured and pre-filed as the 'Secretary of State filings' within the Office of the Secretary of State. As an investor/Member, knowledge of such legal information is indispensable. Again, the emphasis is on compliance and investment valuation. Here, compliance is defined in terms of compliance with the non-profit Association regulatory filings. It is knowledge, authority and compliance of the Association regulatory filings that promotes true investment valuation, not the amenities. Again, the defining legal filings either empower the Association to self-manage or place this authority into the hands of professional Management. Self-education and understanding of these choices assist the investor in making a more informed purchase decision. Such timely education and interaction of the investor is an absolute necessity. Should the nonprofit Association regulatory filings authorize the Association to self-manage, employment of outside professional management not only is a violation of its official fillings, it impose an unnecessary fiscal expense. Again, knowledge of such an interactive decision-making process, further empowers the investor/Member.

An Association with well-informed investor/Members is likely performing according to its fillings. This official operational accountability, characterizing the Association method of operations, is filed within the Office of Secretary of State. Association valuation is impacted by strict compliance with its legal filings character. From a self-education perspective, the investor/Member ought to be well informed of the consequences such legal filings requirement. This Secretary of State filing officially determines who has legal authority to make Association fiscal decisions; the non-profit Association or outside paid professional management.

This predetermined interactive strategy is an inseparable part of the Association operational structure. Too, compliance of the correct regulatory filing framework is central to maintaining nonprofit solvency and nonprofit valuation. Therefore, the investor-Member is well served being pre-informed, rather than post-informed of the Association non-profit legal filings structure as well as the Davis-Stirling Enactment. It is precisely such timely self-education and interaction that protects investment rights and promotes valuation.

Non-profit operations that are counter to the regulatory filings are never acceptable. Legally, a prospective investor of a nonprofit Association is actually entering into a purchase agreement with the "regulatory filings". It is compliance with these legal filings infrastructure that also protects investment valuation. Consequently, an insufficiently informed prospective investor is ill prepared to fully determine associated investment risks. A sufficiently informed investor on the other hand, is able to make a more informed purchasing decision, apart from the very persuasive "dazzling" amenities. Whenever governing, and operational decisions are disjointed from the Association filings structure, it is not the "marketing hype" that assesses risk factors and maintains investment valuation, but rather a working understanding of its regulatory filings requirement, within the Office of Secretary of State. Within this regulatory filing context, correct solutions associated with non-profit issues are highly dependent upon the investor's understanding of this filings infrastructure. Accordingly, just as the California Department of Motor Vehicles driving manual represents the official source to consult for managing driving risks, so too, is the Office of the Secretary of State another agency available to the investor/Member to consult for avoiding investment risks and maintaining investment valuation. Ignorance and non-compliance of the regulatory filings associated with this non-profit lifestyle is never "a good thing".

The Secretary of State regulatory filings, as well as Davis-Stirling legislation, are solution-based resources available to the non-profit investor/Member. Education and compliance of the regulatory filings infrastructure is an empowering resource available to the investor. Conversely, ignorance of these agencies functions redirects authority from control of the investor/Member. Throughout this analysis, the regulatory power is referenced while specifically emphasizing corresponding Civil Codes, illustrations as well as scenarios. All parties are answerable to Davis-Stirling legislation, Association governing Bylaws, and associated agencies for avoiding investment risks, and maintaining investment valuation.

Self-education and compliance of state defined plans protect the prospective owner/investor against market devaluation as well as insolvency, suspension, and even revocation of the Association registered nonprofit status. Ignorance deprives the investor of an effective interaction process, regulatory solutions and legal protection. Within this dynamic framework of the Common Interest Development, it is not just the transfer of "title" into the hand of the investor that confirms ownership and investment security, rather the understanding of Davis-Stirling legislation, Association Bylaws in the form of regulatory filings within the Office of Secretary of State as well as sustained engagement of the investor/Member in the governing process.

within the Office of Secretary of State. Within this self-educational context, governance and management solutions are highly dependent upon the investor's understanding of the Association filings structure.

Scenario

Awesome Association is in the process of hiring new management for the coming fiscal year. Unaware of its non-profit regulatory filings status rights to self-manage, the Association unknowingly relinquished its authority to self-manage its non-profit Association, governing its daily operations. Additionally, this lack of knowledge of its regulatory filings, the Association voted against its regulatory filings, resulting in an unnecessary expense for the Association by incurring and paying for an un-necessary management expense.

This flawed process resulted in the re-election of the old Board. In accordance with the Association own filing status, the Association also relinquished their right to self-govern and self-manage its operations according to its own Secretary of State filings.

Implication: Do Association Board and Member actions demonstrate awareness of its non=profit regulatory filings or the enacted Davis-Stirling *"secret ballot"* mandate?

How does lack of education of Association Bylaws impact Awesome Association's non-profit valuation as well as control of its governing and management decisions?

Davis-Stirling Act

Civil Code 1351

Defined Terms

(a) "Association" means a non-profit corporation, or unincorporated association created for the purpose of managing a common interest development.

(b) "Governing documents" means the declaration, and any other documents such as bylaws, operating rules of the association, and articles of association which govern the operation of the common interest development or association.

Civil Code 1363.03

Election procedures, secret ballots, inspections of elections

(5) Specify a method of selecting one or three independent third parties as inspector, or inspectors, of election utilizing one of the following methods:

(a) Appointment of the inspector, or inspectors by the Board.

(b) Election of the inspector or inspectors by the members of the Association.

(c) Any other method for selecting the inspectors.

(6) Allow the inspector, or inspectors to appoint and oversee additional persons to verify signatures, and to count and tabulate votes as the inspector or inspectors deem appropriate, provided that the persons are independent third parties.

(c) Notwithstanding any other law or provision of the governing documents, elections regarding assessments legally requiring a vote, election and removal of members of the Association Board of directors, amendments to the governing documents, or the grant of exclusive use of common area property pursuant to section 1363.7 shall be held by *secret ballot* in accordance with the procedures set forth in this section. A *quorum* shall be required only if so stated in the governing documents of the Association or other provisions of law. If a quorum is required by the governing documents, each ballot received by the inspector of elections shall be treated as a member present at a meeting for purposes of establishing quorum.

PROFIT or NON- PROFIT

"automatic or stick"

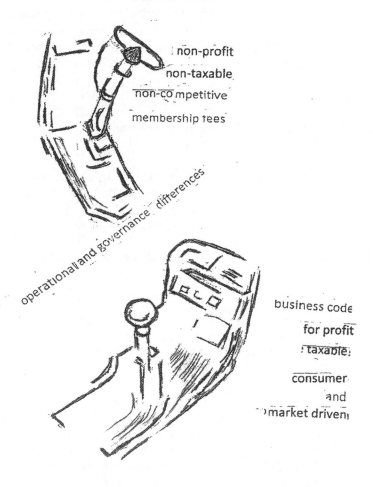

non-profit

non-taxable

non-competitive

membership tees

operational and governance differences

business code

for profit

taxable

consumer

and

market driven

Profit or Non-profit

Automatic or stick

"As a first time home buyer, my reaction to the "for-profit" and "non-profit" corporate concepts, was reactionary, choosing the for-profit model concept over the non-profit model. Who wouldn't choose the well funded managed Association? As a "first time" buyer I wasn't yet aware of structural, strategic, operational and funding differences of the non-profit and for-profit concepts. Are there commonalities? Are there differences? Over lunch, my agent explains the differences from an organization perspective".

Structurally, the non-profit Association is a highly legislated and regulated concept, defined by Davis-Stirling legislation and Association Bylaws filings. Its 501 (C)(3) non-profit status requires Member fees to be reinvested into the Association and used for Association operational expenses. The for-profit infrastructure, on the other hand, is defined by the private enterprise business codes, and not in any way impacted by the Bylaws or Davis-Stirling regulations. Just as the stick shift and automatic transmission structuring not interchangeable, nor are the for-profit and non-profits organizational, operational and funding methods similar, nor are ever interchangeable.

Operationally, both the manual (stick shift) model and the automatic transmission have the capability to transport the motorist from point "A" to "B" while engaging dissimilar methods. So too, are there operational differences between the for-profit Association and non-profit Association. The for-profit Association is regulated by free enterprise business legislation, while the non-profit Association is defined by the structure of its Bylaws filings and Davis-Stirling legislation. Consequently, these operational and legal structural differences impact operational and governing decisions.

Structurally, the Davis-Stirling Act defines the fiscal operations of the non-profit Association 501 (c)(3) non-profit character, while the for-profit Association character is defined by the private enterprise business operations. Just as stick shift and automatic transmission capabilities are non-interchangeable, nor are the funding, taxation and regulatory requirements of the for-profit and non-profit Association ever interchangeable.

Funding for the non-profit business model is obtained by required Member-assessed fees then are required to be reinvested and use for non-profit operations and are non-taxable. The for-profit business model is competitive, driven by profit, and its revenues are taxable. Too, the for-profit business structure is regulated by the private enterprise business code, while the non-profit Association has a 501(c)(3) tax- exempt status, and regulated by the Davis-Stirling Enactment and Bylaws. Finally, the regulatory infrastructure of the for-profit business model is regulated by private enterprise business code, whereas, the non-profit business model infrastructure is regulated by the Davis-Stirling Enactment.

Part of the Board's fiduciary responsibilities is to know prior to hiring, whether or not the managing agent is operating as a non-profit corporation, as well as names and addresses of officers holding interest greater than 10 percent. Ultimately, while year-end financial statements for both for-profit and non-profit models are expected to reflect fiscal sustainability and transparency, their engaging operational and problem solving strategies are different and non-interchangeable.

It is in the best interest of the investor/Member to become self-educated concerning operational differences and requirements prior to finalizing a purchase contract since the IRS requires strict interpretation and execution of *Civil Code* 501(c)(3). Such guidance is priceless in influencing the investor/Member decision- making process. Just as shared Member knowledge can result in collective investment valuation for the non-profit Association, a lack of knowledge can lead to collective investment devaluation. Lack of structural and organizational funding and operational infrastructural differences prior to purchase could prove to be consequential to investment valuation.

Scenario

Amazing Association hires outside vendor Master Management to provide for its accounting and maintenance needs. The Board of Amazing Association also authorizes Master Management to serve as the repository of Association records, as well as intervene on its behalf with city and state agencies, all possibly weakening its operational security of *checks and balances.*

Therefore when Amazing Association fails to file its required state corporate tax return, the Franchise Tax Board automatically shares this default with the Secretary of State, an essential communication link between the two departments regarding the non-profit Association process. This non-compliance action against Amazing Association eventually leads to the suspension of its non-profit status. Only after dismissing Master Management and contracting with Mademoiselle Management does the Association become aware of, and correct this oversight. Had a more acute understanding of the non-profit requirements and Davis-Stirling act been identified, the suspension of the non-profit status hade not occurred.

Implications: Amazing Association is a non-profit concept, impacted by its non-profit model filled Secretary of State filings. Left uncorrected, the consequences of this omission could have lead to the revocation of its non-profit status. What obvious and immediate governance steps is Amazing Association likely correcting? Do you think that Amazing Association is now closely consulting with associated agencies, as well as Davis-Stirling for clarity and guidance in its governing decision making process?

Civil Code 1363.6 Secretary of State Filings

(a) To assist with the identification of common interest developments, each association whether incorporated, or unincorporated shall submit to the Secretary of State on a form, and for a fee not to exceed thirty dollars, that the Secretary of State shall prescribe the following information concerning the association and the development that it manages:

(1) A statement that the Association is formed to manage a common interest development under the Davis-Stirling Common Interest Development Act.

(2) The name of the Association.

(3) The street address of the Association's onsite office, or if none, the responsible officer, or managing agent of the Association.

(4) The name, street address, and daytime telephone number of the president of the Association.

(5) The name, street address, and daytime telephone number of the managing agent, if any.

(6) The county, if in an incorporated area, the city in which the development is physically located.

(7) The nine digit zip code, front street, and nearest cross street of the physical location of the development.

Scenario

According to its Secretary of State filings, All Together Association has the right to self-manage. However, twice during the fiscal year the Association incurred expenses for which it had not sufficiently planned, nor was their any contingency funding addressed.

Implications: How will these unplanned fiscal expenses impact All Together's balance sheet? If such unplanned deficits continue, how will it possibly impact All Together's non-profit status as well as member investment valuation?

Civil Code 1363.1 Managing Agent Disclosures: A prospective agent of a common interest development shall provide a written statement to the board of directors of the association of a common interest development as soon as practicable, but in no event more than 90 days before entering into a management agreement which shall contain the following information concerning the managing agent:

(1) The names and business addresses of the owners, or general partners of the managing agent. If the managing agent is a corporation, the written statement shall include the names and business address of the directors and officers, and shareholders holding greater than 10 percent of the shares of the corporation.

"gps"

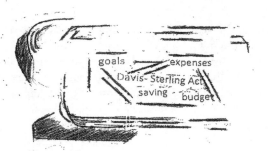

Destination Point

GPS

"This Wednesday night Board meeting agenda: Association fiscal budget. This month personal budget reflects "uncontained" credit card expenses, a small savings balance, and inadequate emergency funding. I can't believe that, yet again, my personal budget is not yet under control".

Many of the same personal expense and saving challenges also impact the non-profit Association budget. However, that said, the regulatory, non-profit structure of the Association is now probed from an offensive planning perspective. Are there any last year expense carried over complicating the current fiscal year process? Is there a need to recapitalize the non-profit Association fiscal budget mid-stream due to insufficient planning? Just as a GPS system provides precise directions for a motorist, so too ought the Association budget, acting as a GPS system, lay out the fiscal direction of the non-profit Association fiscal goals, expenses and cash on hand; thus eliminating the need for any "reactionary fixes". We now therefore, examine the nonprofit Association concept from a planning perspective.

Member assessed monthly fees required for addressing Association fiscal objectives are calculated based on its fiscal expenses. Therefore, the Association fiscal year ought to begin from an offensive planning perspective with an approved budget acting as a fiscal "map". Planning and governing within the non- profit Association are interdependent. Should planning be done retroactively to governing, the Association is set up to underperform, thereby constantly reacting to fiscal challenges. A lack of budget planning therefore, leads to insufficient budget funding which in turn impacts sound governing.

The budget formation is based on preset goals and methods, thus impacting investment valuation. In accordance with the Association regulatory filings, outside Management may or may not be a part of the decision-making process. Accordingly, this budget process is predetermined and cannot be fiscally changed without impacting its Secretary of State refilling. As any motorist has discovered, a successful road trip requires advance planning and the execution of a set of accurately calculated coordinates. Similarly, the non-profit Association is set up to underperform when the governing process is dissociated from the fiscal planning process.

In keeping with our automotive analogy, we come to understand how accurate planning functions as a "global positioning system" as it relates to fiscal goals. *Civil Code 1365* is the GPS system used in making budget determinations. Such precise fiscal planning presets the budgeting coordinates that are In accordance with the non-profit fiscal decisions and governance process. First, GPS coordinates are preset to address any capital expenses identified in the mandatory reserve study. Every three years Davis-Stirling requires a reserve study to be conducted for identifying, and funding capital expenses. Expenses such as extensive plumbing, roof replacement, or elevator remodeling are examples of such capital expenses that should be pre-identified and pre-funded. Ordinary operational expenses are also part of the budget funding process. Summarily, Member assessment dues are calculated based on these budget fundamentals. The governing process should never commence without a fully approved, operational fiscal budget. This detailed planning eliminates any "back and forth" need to re-capitalize, or refund the budget due to ineffective planning.

Incompetent budget planning leads to insufficient budget funding, negatively impacting sound governance and investment valuation.

Our GPS coordinates also pre-determine a timeline for budget distribution to Members. This distribution is due to take place not less than 30 days after, and not more than 90 days prior to the start of the fiscal year. Any variance or non-compliance with this timeline sets the Association up for beginning the governing process either prematurely or belatedly to budgetary funding and distribution. This precise planning must not be omitted or altered by either the Board or professional vendor. The Board, functioning in a decision-making role is responsible for the prioritizing and fiscal budget funding accordingly. Just as sound fiscal planning determines a sound fiscal budget, so too must the governing process be reflective of a sound fiscal budget. The Board, structured from the Association membership, has the last word of approval in accordance with its Association regulatory filings. Again, as long as the governing process is disassociated from a sound budget planning process, the Association budget will continue to be fiscally underfunded, impacting its governing process.

Just as relevant as a well-planned budget, is the import of Member engagement. Member oversight, the governing process and transparency constitute layers of protection impacting investment valuation. For example, should unapproved expenses appear on the Association's account payable ledger, the Membership is always entitled to full disclosure as to why. Should additional funding be required beyond the fiscal budgeted amount, the Board is obligated to justify such expense to the membership in a planned "open meeting". Again, this process is dependent upon the Secretary of State Filings.

This state GPS (Davis-Stirling) is precise in prioritizing and defining goals, methods, timelines, and preparation of the budget. Ultimately, however effectively written, this state GPS is only as effective as the oversight, and engagement of the investor/Member taking the time to educate himself about the fiscal process. Being uninformed is never an option.

Both Board and investor/Member actions must be in agreement with Association regulations. The Board is elected to provide governance leadership based on the Davis-Stirling Act, and the Association Bylaws. The investor/Member, strategically positioned to oversee governing decisions not "break faith" with this regulatory infrastructure pertaining to fiscal budget planning process. There is a direct connection between Association valuation and fiscal planning. It is any surprise that the Board, professional vendor, nor Member gets to take an "off ramp" by relinquishing fiscal duties.

Scenario

Due to deferred maintenance and long term heavy rains, water intrusion severely damages multiple units at Accountable Association. A final bid of $60, 000 is obtained, and presented to the Members for approval 6 months into the fiscal year. Because this expense was not included as part of the mandated contingency planning process, it was necessary to reassess each member $1000 above their regular monthly membership fees to cover this unplanned expense.

Implication: Based on the absence of pre-budgeted reserve funds, is it reasonable to say that the reserve study was not a part of the fiscal budget planning process for Accountable Association? Consequently, would it have been necessary for Accountable Association to assess the membership had contingency planning been a part of the budgeting process? In what ways could this unplanned expenditure impact Accountable Association's budget and balance sheet?

Civil Code 1365 Financial Records and Reporting

Unless the governing documents impose more stringent standards, the association shall do all the following:

(a) A pro forma operating budget, which shall include all of the following:

(1) The estimated revenue and expenses on an accrual basis

(2) A summary of the reserves based upon the most recent review or study conducted pursuant to Section 1365.5, based only on assets held in cash or cash equivalents, which shall be printed in boldface type and include all of the following:

(A) The current estimated replacement cost, estimating remaining life, and estimated useful life of each major component.

(B) As of the end of the fiscal year for which the study is prepared:

(i)   The current estimate of the amount of cash reserves necessary to repair, replace, restore, or maintain the major components.

(ii) The current amount of accumulated cash reserves actually set aside to repair, replace, restore, or maintain major components.

(iii) Instead of complying with the requirements set forth in this clause, an association that is obligated to issue a review of their financial statement pursuant to subdivision (b) may include in the review a statement containing all of the information required by this clause. Notwithstanding a contrary provision in the governing documents, a copy of the operating budget shall be annually distributed not less than thirty days, or not more than ninety days prior to the start of the association's fiscal year.

"kicking the tire"

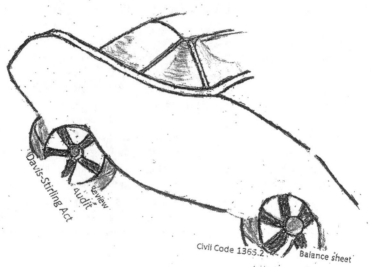

Defensive Stance

Kicking the tires

"The descriptive term "muscle car" creates a vision of advanced technology, power, speed, an exceptional breaking system, high performance tires and a solid body. Such looks and performance equal value"!

Based on its balance sheet data, a non-profit Association value and overall performance are indicators of its solvency prior to filling its annual tax return. Monthly examination of the Association balance sheet will indicate any on going problematic issues. Such timely discoveries enable the Association to assess "assets and debt" and make timely adjustments. As an investor/Member, do you know whether or not the Association is operating within budget? Can you identify problematic issues by examining the balance sheet? As we continue examining the Association fiscal status, we now focus on its solvency by examining the balance sheet and audit report. This fundamental process is yet another option available to assist the Member in determining investment valuation. Is it not obvious that the effectiveness of governing is predicated on the formation of planned budgetary goals, which in turn impact the worth and value of the balance sheet? Just as a pre-planned budget impacts the Association fiscal operations and value, so too, the amount of cash on its balance sheet has a corresponding impact on its investment valuation. Routine maintenance such as tie rotation, oil change, and smog check all facilitate proper functioning of the vehicle. So too, does the importance of detailed examination and maintenance impact the non-profit Association performance. The balance sheet discloses periodic strengths, and weaknesses of the Association performance. The outcome of this process along with budgetary objectives, all confirm and support one another. Too, even a quick income to expense ratio can serve as a financial compass and general indicator of the Association's financial stability. Quarterly scrutiny of the balance sheet provides a dependable trajectory of the Association's worth. Its assets, liabilities and equities should all be documented and made available to Members on a quarterly basis. Finally, since no off balance sheet expenses, including any pertaining to litigations ever excluded, the Association cash balances and liabilities are reliably assessed and disclosed. Conditionally, when Association assets calculations are greater than its liabilities, the quarterly financial condition/strength is considered sound at the time. Therefore, it is possible for an investor/Member to readily determine the given amount of cash on hand or debt by examining the balance sheet. However, it cannot be overly emphasized that the data of one balance sheet is only representative of financial stability or instability at that specified time, in this case quarterly. Ongoing assessment data is required before a conclusive fiscal accounting of valuation and worth is verified. Hence, even with an elected Board in place, Members are empowered with oversight authority to access records and should never be disengaged from the process. Ideally, Members should scrutinize the Association balance sheet on at least a quarterly basis. Keep in mind that document transparency is mandated by Davis-Stirling.

The worth of the investor/Member investment is reflected by the worth and valuation indicated on the Association balance sheet. Too, since the operations of a non-profit organization are mostly conducted on a cash basis, even a Member's unpaid monthly assessment fees together with the Association bank balance and cash on hand are all defined as assets and should be reflected on the balance sheet.

By calculating the difference of the Association total assets, total liabilities [net gain] and strength, [net loss] weakness, is dependable and accurate for only that given time period. Also, the balance sheet data is reliable because no off balance sheet activity is ever permitted. It follows that more frequent examinations and reconciliations of balance sheet data provides a more comprehensive and reliable representation of the Association fiscal condition; hence investment valuation. Should for any reason actual funds are detached from pre-approved funds, the discrepancy appears on the balance sheet. Thus, the value of the balance sheet is a reliable indicator of Association investment valuation for a specific time period.

An additional fiscal tool, the audit may or may not be required as a year-end structural layer for the Association. It too, identifies, protects and confirms Association valuation. Too, this process requires a "hands on" examination of all accounting related documentation including receipts, cancelled checks, credit card debt, litigation expenses, balance sheet reports and the approved budget. This annual process examines, reconciles and validates all Association fiscal statements and transactions. The confirmation of an audit report is provided by the auditor after a comprehensive examination of the accounting records is completed. In the absence of this tangible and comprehensive process, the auditor's signature is withheld from the finished report, rendering the audit unconfirmed. The expressed opinion of the expert conducting the audit must always be affixed to the finished audit report for confirmation. Again, this process requires tangible assess to all records. Only such complete hands on access will determine whether mistakes are material or not. The Association Bylaws, with complete clarity, determines which process is to be use. Should the Association Bylaws review process be in conflict with the state audit process, the Davis-Stirling recommendation is to use the more stringent of the two processes. These completed reports, the year- end audit, or review process reflect the Association fiscal strength or weakness, which in turn impacts the investor/Member investment valuation.

Scenario

During the fiscal year, one of the two elevators at Adaptable Association became inoperable. However, the Board never included this capital expense in the budget contingency planning. To resolve this budgetary short fall, Board members unilaterally decided to authorize Midway Management to substitute the less costly review process for the more stringent, and costly audit process required by the Association bylaws. The decision to change the review process over the more costly audit enabled Adaptable Association in order to pay for the unbudgeted capital expenditure. Was the Board's action justified?

Implication: Because the elevator expense was an unbudgeted expenditure for the Association, it is likely that Board never conducted the reserve study identifying and exposing the potential expense in a timely manner.

Civil code 1365.5 Financial Duties of Board; Reserve Transfers

    (a) Unless the governing documents impose more stringent standards, the board of directors of the Association shall do all of the following:

    (2) Review a current reconciliation of the association's reserve account on at least a quarterly basis.

    (3) Review on at least a quarterly basis, the current year's actual reserve revenues and expenses compared to the current year's budget.

    (4) Review the latest account statements prepared by the financial institutions where the association has its operating and reserve accounts.

    (5) Review an income and expense statement for the association's operating and reserve accounts on at least a quarterly basis.

    (f) As used in this section, "reserve accounts" means both of the following:

    (1) Money that the association's board of directors has identified for use to defray the future repair or replacement of, or additions to, those major components which the association is obligated to maintain.

(g) As used in this section, "reserve account" requirements means the estimated funds which the Association's board of directors has determined are required to be available at a specified point in time to repair, replace, or restore those major components which the association is obligated to maintain.

Scenario

A potential investor looking to invest in a non-profit Association has narrowed his consideration to two choices Awkward Association, and Applause Association. Both Associations meet the requirements of the potential investor with regard to location, square footage and monthly assessment fees. However, only Applause Association is able to consistently provide requested copies of financial reports, and statements such as the balance sheet, annual audit, budget plans and reserve study for the past two years.

Implication: Which of the two sales listings is the investor likely to choose, and which listing is likely to cause both fiscal and valuation problems for the Association?

Civil Code 1365.2 Inspection of Books and Records

(a) For the purpose of this section, the following definitions apply:

(1) "Association records" means all of the following:

(A) Any financial document required to be provided to a member in Section 1365

(B) Any financial document or statement required to be provided in Section 1368

(C) Intern financial statements, or as compiled, containing any of the following:

(i) Balance sheet

(ii) Income and expense statement

(iii) Budget comparison

(c)

(1) The Association shall make the specified Association records available for inspection, and copying in the Association's business office within the common area development.

(2) If the Association does not have a business office within the development, the Association SHALL make the specified association records available for inspection and copying in a place that the requesting member and the Association agree upon.

Tax Reporting

"fiscal millage"

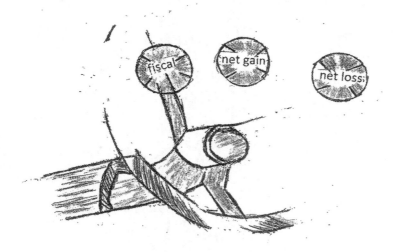

Tax Reporting

Fiscal mileage

"Without a doubt", tax filing is not among my most up beat things to do. Experience has taught me however, to save every receipt impacting the annual process. Family medical expenses are higher this year because of a flu outbreak as well as needed physical therapy for my son's sport's injuries. Overall, my record keeping has improved "some what". This will make my accountant's day."

From a reporting perspective, the final fiscal accountability of the non-profit Association is its annual tax filing. However, the fiscal requirement is not an isolated process. This year-end exit process represents the cumulative impact of the budget, the strength or weakness of each balance sheet, the impact of every non-profit policy violation, each fiscal challenge, as well as any litigation expenses. The cumulative impact of each fiscal decision defines and validates the valuation of the non-profit Association in terms of "dollars and cents". Clearly, it is the aggregate application of fiscal decisions based on the Association By-laws and Davis-Stirling Enactment and financials that impact the non-profit Association. Initially, this non-profit fiscal journey began by posing a direct question to the prospective investor/Member: Do you understand the non-profit characterization of the Association? In response the tenor of the discussion examined the non-profit concept, Enactment of Davis-Stirling, Bylaws, financial records, fiscal funding, decisions and their cumulative impact on investment valuation. At this juncture, the "fiscal odometer" indicates that the Association is positioned to disengage from the fiscal year by filing the annual tax return. This final process, remittance of the non-profit Association tax return involves the accumulative disclosure of all fiscal reports in order to evaluate its non-profit worth. Accordingly, emphasis shifts from regulatory strategies in the forms of election, fiscal planning, governing, mediating and assessing to that of an exit perspective, the tax return filling. Summarily, the results of this year- end process confirms the effectiveness of the non-profit fiscal planning, decision making, record keeping, as well as governing which in turn impact investment valuation.

Should the Association's gross income collected from Member fees exceeds $75,000, each Member automatically receive a copy of the Association tax return within 120 days after the closing fiscal year. Regulations also require that a state licensee prepare the tax return in accordance with the California Board of Accountancy standards. Too, a qualifying Association can file for a special election, exempting membership fees from taxation. It is the 501(c)(3) non-profit Association status allowing for this exemption. This level of fiscal accountability and transparency, when strictly enforced, directly impacts investment valuation. It is established law mandating the fiscal process and providing investor/Member access to records and transparency. Such strict compliance impacts investment valuation as well as the 501(c)(3) status of the non-profit Association.

Prior to beginning any road trip, the motorist is expected to exercise appropriate driving skills, maintain the automobile in good operating condition, and comply with all state driving regulations. Why? The state has concluded that if these issues are preaddressed, fiscal problems are minimized. This same strategic planning is foundational for operations of non-profit Association dwelling. Prior to and certainly during the first year, the investor should become familiar with the processes of planning, governance, record keeping, and reporting related to non-profit Association infrastructure. An investor/Member understanding of the non-profit fiscal process impacts the success of both immediate and long-term investment valuation. When strictly adhered to, the Davis-Stirling and Secretary of State Fillings structures minimize investment devaluation, perhaps avoiding fiscal complications altogether. The remittance of the tax return speaks to fiscal success and or failure, and or threats as they relate to compliance of the Association internal controls; The Davis-Stirling Enactment and its Bylaws. The non-profit Association, Davis-Stirling Enactment, and informed investor/ Members: a "winning team".

Scenario

Mindful Management provided accounting and management services for Afterthought Association. Three months after the tax filing, a Member requested a completed copy of the Association's tax return, hoping to learn about the status of the Association's reserve funding account. The Member was stunned to discover that not only was the Association reserve funding was undisclosed, but also that the return was not signed by an officer of the Board, or a tax professional.

Implication: Without the required signatures, is the tax return filing considered a legal tax document? Would the IRS be inclined to accept or reject an uncertified tax filing? Do these omissions inspire confidence concerning other documentation prepared by Mindful Management?

*Civil Code 1365.5*Financial Duties of Board; Reserve Transfers

(a) Unless the governing documents impose more stringent standards, the board of directors of the association shall do all of the following:

(1) Review a current reconciliation of the association's reserve account on at least a quarterly basis.

(2) Review a reconciliation of the association's operating accounts on at least a quarterly basis.

(3) Review on a quarterly basis the current year's actual reserve revenues and expenses compared to the current year's budget.

(4) Review the latest account statements prepared by the financial institutions where the association has its operating and reserve accounts.

(5) Review an income and expense statement for the association's operating and reserve accounts on at least a quarterly basis.

(b) The signatures of at least two persons, who shall be members of the association's board of directors, or one officer who is not a member of the board of directors, and a member of the board of directors shall be required for the withdrawal of moneys from the association's reserve accounts.

Scenario

Marvelous Management has successfully acquired a contract with Adorable Association. Contract conditions specifically allow Marvelous Management to provide accounting, maintenance, as well as tax preparation services. Adorable Association was extremely pleased with the tremendous accuracy and savings produced. Marvelous Management was also persuasive in convincing Adorable Association to substitute its costly annual audit mandated by the Association Bylaws, for the less expensive review process in contrary to its Bylaws. The reasoning for the changes was to reduce Association fiscal expenses.

Implication: Though well intended, without a more stringent protective system of checks and balances in place, is the reporting confirmation and verification processes compromised? Does the Association decision to substitute the annual audit for the less expensive review process a violation? Without first amending and filing new structural change(s) to Adorable Association Bylaws, is the Association in compliance within its official requirements?

Civil Code 1365 Financial Records and Reporting

Unless the governing documents impose more stringent standards, the association shall prepare and distribute to all of its members the following documents:

(a) A pro forma operating budget, which shall include all of the following:

(1) The estimated revenue and expenses on an accrual basis.

(2) A summary of the association's reserves based upon the most recent review or study conducted pursuant to Section 1365.5, based only on assets held in cash or each equivalents, which shall be printed in boldface type and include all of the following:

(A) The current estimated replacement cost, estimated remaining life, and estimated useful life of each major component.

(B) As of the end of the fiscal year for which the study is prepared:

(i) The current estimate of the amount of cash reserves necessary to repair, replace, restore, or maintain the major components.

(ii) The current amount of accumulated cash reserves actually set aside to repair, replace, restore, or maintain major components.

The summary of the association's reserves disclosed pursuant to paragraph (2) shall not be admissible in evidence to show improper financial management of an association, provided that other relevant and competent evidence of the financial condition of the association is not made inadmissible by this provision.

Notwithstanding a contrary provision in the governing documents, a copy of the operating budget shall be annually distributed not less than 30 days nor more than 90 days prior to the beginning of the association's fiscal year.

(b) A review of the financial statement of the association shall be prepared in accordance with generally accepted accounting principles by a licensee of the California Board of Accountancy for any fiscal year in which the gross income to the association exceeds seventy-five thousand dollars ($75,000). A copy of the review of the financial statement shall be distributed within 120 days after the close of each fiscal year.

Civil Code 1365.2 Inspection of Books and Records

(a) For the purposes of this section, the following definitions shall apply:

(1) "Association records" means all of the following:

(A) Any financial document required to be provided to a member in Section 1365.

(B) Any financial document or statement required to be provided in Section 1368.

(C) Interim financial statements, periodic or as compiled, containing any of the following:

    (i)   Balance sheet

    (ii) Income and expense statement

    (iii) Budget comparison

    (iv) General ledger. A "general ledger" is a report that shows all transactions that occurred in an association account over a specified period of time. The records described in this sub-paragraph shall be prepared in accordance with an accrual or modified accrual basis of accounting.

(D) Executed contracts not otherwise privileged under law.

(E) Written board approval of vendor or contractor proposals or invoices.

(F) State and federal returns

(G) Reserve account balances and records of payments made from reserve accounts

Injunctive Relief

"penalty"

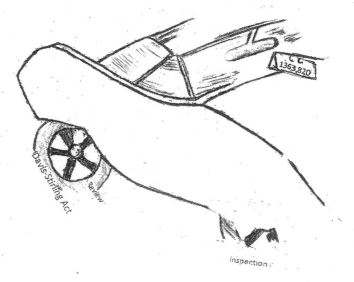

Davis-Stirling Act

Review

1363.820

inspection

Injunctive Relief

Penalty

"I recall my agent saying the traditional judicial system isn't the only option for the Member/investor to address internal grievances. Davis-Stirling empowers the investor/Member to apply the "regulatory breaks", and resolve issues without cost. From a mediatory perspective, the investor/Member is empowered with an option to avoid legal expenses. We now examine the non-profit process from a mediatory perspective".

Within the Department of Consumer Affairs, the Member has access to a remediation process, if desired and without legal expense for resolving internal conflicts. Once again, the regulatory structure of Davis-Stirling provides an option for controlling expenses for the Association and Member. Upon written request, the Board, not Management is obligated to "meet and confer" about internal issues. Such proceedings and their outcome are dated, stamped and memorialized in writing as part of the Association record.

Within this non-profit environment, solutions are not predicated on the dynamics of personal charisma and style of a particular Board. Though the Board serves in a position of guidance, it is imperative that each investor/Member become educated about processes related to planning, governing, as well as options for resolving internal conflict. Again, such a process demonstrates the effectiveness of Davis-Stirling to control fiscal expenses impacting valuation and avoiding costly litigious conflict.

Illiteracy of Davis-Stirling regulations is defeating to operations and governance processes, thus impacting investor/Member valuation. No investor/Member has to standby helplessly observing and accepting harmful practices to his investment valuation without redress. The investor/Member has the right to "meet and confer" with the Board regarding problematic governance, and operational issues impacting the Association. By invoking *Civil Code 1363.820*, a Member is empowered to effectively challenge methods and decisions by first initiating a good faith dialogue. Once initiated, all involved parties are legally obligated to participate in this dispute resolution process. This can be done with or without a third party present and prior to any request for traditional outside judicial intervention.

On the other hand, should either party fail to "meet and confer" once the procedure is invoked, non-participation is legally recorded as default. You wouldn't want to default on payment to your auto mechanic once he's completed any required maintenance on your car, would you? Enforcement action for declaratory, injunctive, or writ relief is initiated by invoking *Civil Code 1369.530*. Procedures for these alternative dispute resolution procedures require court intervention.

Should a motorist persist in violating California driving regulations, points against his driving record can result in greater fines, license suspension, or maybe permanent revocation of a driver's license.

Similarly, disciplinary actions impacting an Association can range from fines, suspension, or revocation of its 501(c) (3) non-profit status resulting in re-characterization of the non-profit regulatory infrastructure. Under deregulation, Member assessment fees would become taxable, investor/Member property equity, and valuation would be impacted differently by both taxation, and insurance premium cost. Such changes would re-define the Common Interest Development regulatory infrastructure.

Remember, the non-profit concept is unique because of its legal characterization set forth within the Secretary of State filing. Therefore, non-compliance is never an option. Whether functioning in the capacity of a governing Board, investor/Member, or vendor for the non-profit Association; such alliances automatically establish an operating and governing contract with the enactment of Davis-Stirling. Upon breach of faith with Association Bylaws, Articles of Incorporation, Davis-Stirling Act, or Secretary of State filings, an investor/Member is empowered to enforce corrective actions either by initiating mediation, or the alternative dispute resolution process as a solution based strategy. The acting Board is compelled to participate and even subject to recall should it become necessary.

Scenario

Part 1

The Board of Advancement Association imposed a $2,000 assessment on each of its Members prior to notice or meaning discussions. The purpose of the extra funding was to be used for common area maintenance expense. A Member complained, alerting the Board via first class mail, that the Davis-Stirling Act does not support unilateral governing and decision-making actions in the absence of investor/Member input and vote.

Implication: Do you think that the Board was knowledgeable of Member rights relating to scheduled meetings, Member involvement, as well as disclosure of a fiscal budget, balance sheet assessments, and minutes?

Civil Code 1363.820 Requirement for adoption of reasonable internal dispute resolution procedure.

(a) An association shall provide a fair, reasonable, and expeditious procedure for resolving a dispute within the scope of this article.

(b) In developing a procedure pursuant to this article, an association shall make maximum, reasonable use of available local dispute resolution programs involving a neutral third party, including low-cost mediation programs such as those listed on the Department of Consumer Affairs, and the United States Department of Housing and Urban Development websites.

(c) If an association does not provide a fair, reasonable, and expeditious procedure for resolving a dispute within the scope of this article, the procedure provided in Section 1363.840, default internal dispute resolution procedure and applies, and satisfies the requirement of subdivision.

Scenario

Part 2

Having waited well over two months without a response from the Board, the Member requested to meet and confer regarding the conflict. The Member also requested the presence and participation of a neutral third party. Within the context of the internal dispute resolution process, the issue was successfully resolved. It was determined that the Board had exceeded its authority by imposing an assessment without Member involvement and documentation.

Civil code 1363.840 Default Internal Dispute Resolution Procedure

(a) This section applies in an association that does not otherwise provide a fair, reasonable, and expeditious dispute resolution procedure.

(b) Either party to the dispute within the scope of this article may invoke the following procedure:

(1) The party may request the other party to meet and confer in an effort to resolve the dispute. The request shall be in writing.

(2) A member of an association may refuse to meet and confer. The association may not refuse to meet and confer.

(3) The association board of directors shall designate a member of the board to meet and confer.

(4) The parties shall meet promptly.

(5) A resolution of the dispute agreed to by the parties shall be memorialized in writing and signed by the parties.

(c) An agreement reached under this section binds the parties and is judicially enforceable if:

(1) The agreement is not in conflict with law or the governing documents of the common interest development or association.

(d) A member of the association may not be charged a fee to participate in the process.

Civil code 1369.520 Pre-litigation Alternative Dispute Resolution

(a) An association or an owner or a member of a common interest development may not file an enforcement action in the Superior Court unless the parties have endeavored to submit their dispute to alternative dispute resolution pursuant to this article.

(b) This section applies only to an enforcement action that is solely for declaratory, injunctive, or writ relief, or for that relief in conjunction with a claim for monetary damages not is excess of five thousand dollars ($5,000).

(c) This action does not apply to a small claims action.

(d) Except as otherwise provided by law, this section does not apply to an assessment dispute.

Civil code 1369.530 Initiating ADR

(a) Any party to a dispute may initiate the process required by Section 1369.520 by serving on the parties to the dispute a request for resolution. The request for resolution shall include all of the following:

(1) A brief description of the dispute between the parties.

(2) A request for alternative dispute resolution.

(3) A notice that the party receiving the request for resolution is required to respond within 30 days or receipt of the request will be deemed rejected.

(4) If the party on whom the request is served is the owner of a separate interest, a copy of this article

Bess Caldwell

(b) Service of the request for resolution shall be by personal delivery, first class mail, express mail, facsimile transmission, or other means reasonably calculated to provide the party on whom the request is served actual notice of the request.

(c) A party on whom a request for resolution is served has 30 days following service to accept or reject the request. If a party does not accept the request within the period, the request is deemed rejected by the party.

Civil code 1369.540 ADR deadlines

(a) If the party on whom a request for resolution accepts the request, the parties shall complete the alternative dispute resolution within 90 days after the party initiating the request receives the acceptance, unless this period is extended by written stipulation signed by the parties.

(b) Chapter 2 (commencing with Section 1115) of Division 9 of the Evidence Code applies to any form of alternative dispute resolution initiated by a request for resolution under this article other than arbitration.

(c) The costs of the alternative dispute resolution shall be borne by the parties.

"Classic"

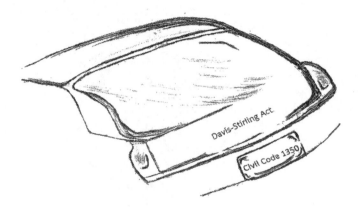

Investment Outlook

Classic test drive

"Are we there yet"? Had we been disciplined to stay with the "planned rout", we could have avoided the speeding and parking fines. From a non-profit investment perspective, the overriding question becomes: What regulatory and operational guidance are in place controlling risks and deficits?"

Davis-Stirling Regulations provide a multi-layered protective infrastructure that facilitates guidance, and investment valuation. Did the non-profit Association have a fiscal plan? How would you evaluate the fiscal year performance? Did the Association fiscal decisions maintain, increase, or decrease investment valuation? The confluence of regulatory infrastructures control risks and deficits impacting the Association's non-profit character, its vision, and fiscal success. How would you assess your non-profit Association fiscal year"?

Long-term investment/valuation is conditional upon the investor/ Member understanding of Davis-Stirling Enactment, as well as continued involvement in Association "day to day" operations. Any unauthorized business model in conflict with Davis-Stirling regulations significantly devalues the non-profit character, thus impacting investment valuation. On the other hand, active participation, compliance of Davis-Stirling, and Association Bylaws constitute winning strategies for effectively controlling risks, thus promoting solvency and valuation.

Each investor/Member has oversight authority pertaining to processes of election, budgeting, governing, operating, mediating recalling, and record disclosure. Regulations define the common purpose and goals of the non-profit Association, but it is active involvement of the investor/Member that preserves long-term valuation. Think of the overall fiscal process this way: Davis-Stirling compliance impacts overall fiscal planning which impacts the strength or weakness of the balance sheet, which in turn impacts the outcome of federal and state tax return filings, which in turn impacts the audit report, which ultimately impacts the Secretary of State filing and investment valuation. These are the fundamentals defining the non-profit fiscal equation, hence its long term vision and success. Davis-Stirling is the master mechanic that keeps your "vehicle on the road", enabling the Member/investor to maneuver through the fiscal processes of electing, planning, governing, reporting, and assessing fiscal reports, adjudicating conflict, thus enforcing legislation. Such governing and managing infrastructures demand that the investor/Member become self-educated. Such self-education impact any flawed decisions impacting the non-profit Association performance and valuation.

The Board, elected from among the membership has a fiduciary duty to govern within these pre-defined state infrastructures. The Association President chairs Board meetings while the treasurer prepares monthly financial reports. Funding of fiscal obligations is accomplished through mandatory Member fees and deposited into the Association treasure under the stewardship of the Treasurer. The Secretary is responsible for preservation of accurate minutes. In accordance with the regulatory fillings, oversight authority may or may not be tactically placed in the hand of the investor/Member. Within this non-competitive, apolitical, self-governing infrastructure, the non-profit Association is structured to be highly successful in deterring self-serving interests, thus promoting investment valuation.

The luminaries of this visionary concept further minimized investment risks, characterizing the Association as non-profit, requiring all assets to be reinvested into the Association. This process makes active participation and oversight of the investor/Member all the more critical. When governing and operational duties are performed in accordance with established law, valuation is maintained, protecting the Association non-profit status. Lack of Member/investor understanding of Davis-Stirling Legislation, and Member/investor oversight, serves only to de-leverage Member/investor control, and investment valuation; conceding governing and management control to unintended interests. Unauthorized and self-serving governing and management responsibilities can only devalue investment interests, solvency and sustainability.

Just as state driving regulations promote a safe operational environment for motorists, so too, do the fundamentals of Davis-Stirling Enactment together with Association Bylaws and associated agencies help promote non-profit investment goals and sustainability. It cannot be overstated: Member self-education and active engagement is indispensable for ensuring viability and long-term demand of the non-profit industry. Why? The Member/investor is not simply purchasing real estate, but is actually entering into a contractual agreement with the Davis-Stirling Act, Association Bylaws, and associated agencies. From a long- term investment perspective, it is self-education, and compliance that provide the necessary leverage for protecting investment valuation. As a Member/investor, have you grasped the statue of this non-profit concept? Are you actively involved in the non-profit Association fiscal processes?

Having taken a forensic look at the non-profit infrastructures, findings are clear. Investment valuation is contingent upon complete compliance of Davis-Stirling and Association Bylaws. Clearly, the Common Interest Development concept, known as the non-profit Association, Davis-Stirling and the Member/investor are indivisible. Yes, the compliance of Davis-Stirling, Association Bylaws, and the educated Member/investor constitute the "under the hood" engine impacting investment valuation; a winning formula!

Scenario

Based on prior fiscal budget funding projections, Adjustable Association prefunded its capital reserve account in order to manage emergency contingences. This pre-funding process is a mandate of the Davis-Stirling Act. Three months into the fiscal year, a safety issue with its standpipes was discovered during the city mandatory safety testing process. This testing process was conducted by the city fire department. Test results indicated that the water-flow pressure did not meet regulated psi pressure standards needed to extinguish a fire.

Implication: A significant fiscal emergency could have occurred had Adjustable Association not pre-planned for unforeseen contingences during the budgeting process. This is but one example why reserve funding is required.

Adjustable Association

Operating Budget
February 1, 2014- January 31, 2015

Operating Income	Monthly	Annual
Association Dues	$32,450	$444,400
Laundry Income	600	7,200
Total Operating Income	**$33,050**	**$451,600**
	Operating Expenses	
Contract Services		
Insurance: Earthquake, Fire, Liability	$9,000	$108,000
Insurance: Workers Comp	300	3,600
Management Contract	800	9,600
Landscaping Contract	1,000	12,000
Elevator Contract	500	6,000
Pest Control	300	3,600

TOTAL CONTRACT SERVICES	**$12,200**	**$146,400**
Utilities		
Electricity	$3,500	$42,000
Natural Gas	6,000	72,000
Water	2,000	24,000
Sewage	400	4,800
Waste Removal	900	10,800
Telephone	300	1,800
TOTAL UTILITIES	**$13,100**	**$157,200**
Maintenance Services		
Plumbing	$300	$3,600
Roof	300	3,600
Maintenance Employee	2,600	31,200
Electrical	100	1,200
Doors/Gates	200	2,400
Painting	150	1,800
HVAC	500	6,000
Gutters/Downspouts	100	1,200
Locks/Keys	50	600
Building Supplies	400	4,800
Fire Protection	100	1,200
Intercom	100	1,200
Security	200	2,400
General Repairs	800	9,600
TOTAL MAINTENANCE	**$5,900**	**$70,800**
Administrative		
Office/Admin Expense	$150	$1,800
Payroll Processing	100	1,200
Postage	100	1,200

Payroll Taxes	200	2,400
Legal	300	3,600
Accounting: Monthly	700	8,400
Accounting: Annually	350	4,200
Licenses	40	480
Employee Mileage	100	1,200
Miscellaneous	100	1,200
TOTAL ADMINISTRATIVE	**$2,140**	**$25,680**
TOTAL OPERATING EXPENSES	**$33,340**	**$400,080**
OPERATING SURPLUS BEFORE RESERVE FUNDING		
Reserve Funding		
Monthly Reserve Contribution	$793.33(12)	$9,519.96
Standpipes Funding	3,500(12)	42,000
TOTAL RESERVE FUNDING	**$4,293.33**	
NET OPERATING SURPLUS	_____	_____

Glossary of Terms

Accountability- Demonstration of responsibility

Association – Shared investment interests of the investors.

Balance Sheet – Method displaying accountability of expenses and cash on hand must.

Board – A group of Members chosen by the Members in the electoral process; President,

Bylaws– Association rules and regulations enacted and filed with the Office of Secretary of State.

authority regarding the process, decision -making process is predetermined

filed. Whether or not this binding authority rests in the hand of Management or the

Association Board is legally determined at this juncture, before the sales process begins

Budget – Allocation of approved fiscal funds by the invested Member for achieve and reinvested into the Association for the operations and maintenance needs.

Common Area – An area of the Association used in common by Members. Example; pool, barbecue area, and hot tub.

Davis-Stirling Act – State Legislation written by former governor Grey Davis for the operation and management of the non-profit Association.

Deficit- Negative cash flow

Devalue- To be undervalued

Fiscal period - The official beginning and closing cycles of a business. Ex. The fiscal period for Summer Time Association is September15.

Infrastructure- Internal organizing and structuring

Management – Method of conducting business.

Member- An owner-member of the nonprofit Association

Monetize - Conversion of an idea into value and capital

Non Profit Organization – Organization funds are exempt from taxation when funds are reinvested back into the organization.

Perspective - Point of view

Profit - Growth

Regulations – Rules enacted by the State.

Recall-A process to de-seat a Board Member

Solvency- Financially sound

Sustainability- Capable of continuing and enduring

Regulatory Fillings – Legal rules and regulations filled for the official structural operations of a Corporation.

Strategy - Strategic- plan.

Valuation - The worth and value assigned or perceived

Closing

We all look forward to that day when our dream of home ownership becomes a reality. We don't want that dream to become a nightmare. This book serves as a guide to help you avoid common pitfalls that can occur when living in a home governed by rules and regulations set in place by a home owner association. With careful thought, education, and planning, your dream home will be everything you envisioned... even better!

Resources

Davis-Stirling information: www.Davis-Stirling.com

Download the Davis-Stirling Act: http://Cardinal-online.com/wp-Content/uploads/2011/06/Davis-Stirling-Act-2012.pdf

California Civil Code: www.leginfo.Ca.gov/.html/
Civ_table_of_contents.html

California legislative information code search: www.leginfo.
legislative.ca.gov

Printed in the United States
By Bookmasters